Great Monsters of the Movies

Great Monsters of the Movies

by Edward Edelson

Doubleday & Company, Inc.
Garden City, New York

791.43
Ede

ISBN: 0-385-00668-3 Trade
        0-385-00857-0 Prebound
Library of Congress Catalog Card Number 72–87499
Copyright © 1973 by Edward Edelson
9 8 7 6 5 4 3

Table of Contents

The Legends   1

The Pioneers   21

Three Frightening Men   31

The Big Beasts   55

A Miscellany of Monsters   71

Index   99

Great
Monsters
of the Movies

The Legends

Everyone loves a monster.

At first, that doesn't sound right. After all, isn't everyone supposed to be afraid of a monster? But it is a strange kind of fear that sends adults and children by the millions into libraries and movie theaters in search of tales of terror. It is the same feeling that makes children scream with pleasure on a spinning, diving rise at the carnival. Obviously, there is something deep down inside most people that gets pleasure out of sheer fright.

This "something" seems to go back to the very beginning of human history. The oldest civilizations man has known have all had their frightening tales of ghosts and other unearthly creatures. It is safe to say that tales designed to send a chill down the listener's spine go back even farther, to the earliest, unrecorded days of mankind. And today, of course, that same "something" has helped make the monster one of the most popular screen characters.

You can understand this deep-down feeling better by thinking of the earliest days, when primitive men had just begun to master the talents that led to civilization. There they sit at night, huddled around a small, flickering fire surrounded by darkness and frightening noises. Almost anything could be out there in that darkness, and—in the mind of primitive man—almost anything could happen at any time. Perhaps a man could turn into an animal or back again. Perhaps a sorcerer could make a spirit rise and obey him. Perhaps the dead could come back to plague the living. And certainly, huge, monstrous animals could suddenly plunge out of the forest to create havoc. The world was new and hard to explain.

One way of explaining it was to invent tales about the beings who controlled all these strange events—for to the mind of primitive man, every event was controlled by beings that were like humans, only much more powerful. These tales were intended not to frighten people but to soothe them. Passed from generation to generation, these stories soon became traditional parts of a culture.

Perhaps that is how tales of horror began. We will never know for sure. But we do know that they have continued to be part of human culture to this day—perhaps not a highly respected part in modern times, but one that continues to feel a real human need. In primitive times, tales and legends had a religious purpose, since every aspect of the primitive man's life was filled with magic. Only later did entertainment become the main purpose of tales of terror. Today, some people in undeveloped areas of the world may hold on to the deeper, magic significance of their horror tales. But in this country, horror stories and movies are only pure entertainment, an attempt to escape for a while from the dull, everyday world into a setting where almost anything can happen and all the old terrors are loose again, if only for a few hours.

In the beginning, monster stories were told by bards who recited the tales they had memorized. Later came the written word, which allowed these tales to be put on paper. Today, the real home of the monster story is the movie theater. That is where the terror seems most realistic and delicious.

It is easy to understand why monsters are so much at home in the movies. For one thing, when you go to the movies you sit in the dark, and darkness is a sheltering, comfortable home for monsters. (It is even more frightening to read a mystery story at home alone after dark than to read it in broad daylight.) Then again, a motion picture can show you, in vivid, realistic detail, all the terrors that you could care to imagine. In the movies an "impossible" happening suddenly becomes ordinary: a vampire turns into a bat in front of your eyes, a man-made monster rises up and walks, a respectable businessman is transformed into a hairy wolf in a few seconds, a huge ape destroys a city as you watch in fascination. Even in these sophisticated days, there is something very magical about watching the impossible come true on the screen.

But the movies can also do just the opposite, and make an ordinary event into a frightening, sinister happening. A clever director can turn the most common, everyday scene into something you shudder at. For example, consider a scene that shows a living room that could be in your house. Weird music starts, a door creaks, curtains billow with the wind, a telephone rings and no one answers— almost all these things happen every night at home, but when they happen on the screen, under the proper direction, they can be more frightening than a bucket of blood.

In fact, many of the most frightening movies rely more on hints and indirect actions than they do on actual pictures of terrifying beings doing awful things. It does not take much skill to scare people by showing a scene with a lot of gore. Just the opposite; these scenes usually end up by boring the viewer because they are so monotonous. The real talent is the ability to make you scream with pleasant fright and hide your face from nothing more than a shadow moving across the screen. The great directors do that, using the scenes of out-and-out horror to bring the movie to a climax. Only in the movies can the ordinary be used to set the scene for moments of wild fright.

And, of course, movie background music helps—slinky, scary music that goes with all the monstrous happenings on the screen. Background music started in the days when movies were silent, and every theater had a piano player or an organist who would play tunes that helped set the mood of each scene—fast music for chases, funny music for comedies, and so on. When talking pictures arrived, the practice of providing music to build the mood of a picture continued, but now the music was added to the sound track at the studio.

There is no question that a few chords can heighten the terror of a monster movie. But too often, frightening music is used as a substitute for good acting and direction. It is too easy to overdo background music, and some of the greatest monster movies use almost no music at all. But to most moviegoers, no scene of terror is quite complete without the right background of minor chords.

It might be thought that the television screen is an even better medium for terror than a movie theater, but it usually doesn't work that way. Most people watch television at home, surrounded by all the familiar belongings that make terror on the screen less realistic. Since the television screen is small, nothing on it is quite as convincing as what you see on the bigger-than-life movie screen. And while a motion picture goes on without interruption, allowing the director to build a mood of terror, most television programs are interrupted frequently for advertisements. Somehow, it is hard to be truly frightened when a monster scene is followed by a deodorant commercial. Finally, if you do get scared, you can turn to another channel, something that is impossible in the movies. While there have been some successful attempts at television terror, the movies remain the real stamping ground of the great monsters.

Because movie monsters are so popular, writers, producers, and directors have scoured the world's folk tales and literature to come up with enough unearthly creatures to meet the demand. Monsters of every variety, some traditional, some modern inventions, have been created in movie studios for the benefit of waiting horror fans.

One of the most durable movie monsters is the vampire, a repulsive creature that goes far back in human history.

Many ancient peoples, including the Egyptians and the Greeks, had folk tales of "undead" men who rose from the grave and needed human blood for their food. In more recent times, these legends have come to center in southeastern Europe—more specifically, in a picturesque province of Romania called Transylvania, which is near the Hungarian border. It is in this part of Europe that the vampire legend has become most highly developed, with a wealth of details covering every aspect of a vampire's life, habits, and death.

According to these legends, the true vampire is neither quite alive nor quite dead. He—or it—is something in between, and chilling. There are several ways of becoming a vampire, all of them terrifying; the most common is to be bitten by another vampire.

Once the vampire comes into existence—"born" is the wrong word—he must sleep in his own closed coffin during the daytime. When night falls, the legend says, the vampire goes out to seek the blood that sustains him. The vampire ordinarily prefers sleeping victims. Sneaking up on them, he sinks his teeth into the neck, draining just enough blood to keep the victim alive. The vampire does not let emotions interfere with his cravings; a woman who is unlucky enough to fall in love with a vampire is likely to be his first victim.

Legend gives the vampire the ability to turn himself into unhuman forms—a wisp of mist perhaps, or (more often) a bat. It is remarkable to note that there actually is such a creature as a vampire bat, found in Latin America, which does live on blood. The vampire bat is far less sinister than the legendary vampire, however. It is a small creature that usually preys on cattle or other animals, biting them and then lapping up the blood as it flows from the wound. Only occasionally will a vampire bat feed on a human, and then it does not bite the throat but usually the big toe. Vampire bats are more a nuisance than a horror.

The ability of the legendary vampire to transform himself into mist or animal enables him to go many places where an ordinary man could not, and to escape from certain traps. On occasion, when his enemies are closing in, the vampire is reputed to turn himself into a wolf for swift escape.

While these supernatural powers make the vampire a formidable enemy, the legend also says they have many weak spots that leave them open to attack. For example, daylight is death to a vampire. He must be back in his coffin by the time the sun rises, for he will die when the sunlight strikes him. And it must be his own coffin; no other will do.

For some reason, garlic is another weapon against the vampire. The legends say that vampires cannot bear the smell of garlic, and so superstitious folk rub garlic on their doorsills and windows at night to keep vampires away. And because the vampire is an unholy creature, it can be destroyed by holy water and it flees from a crucifix or anything shaped like a cross.

To kill a vampire, only a few selected weapons will do. A silver bullet will slay the vampire, but an ordinary bullet will not. The most effective method of eliminating a vampire is to drive a stake through its heart, preferably with a single blow. Some versions of the legends say that the stake must never be removed, or the vampire will return to life. Another vampire disposal method is to burn the coffin that is his resting place. Left without a home, the vampire will perish when the sun rises. However, the legends add that vampires are keenly aware of this danger, and so they hide their coffins with great care.

While there have been many works of fiction on the vampire theme, most vampire movies have been based on the novel *Dracula*, which was written in 1897 by a British author named Bram Stoker. It was this novel that placed the homeland of vampires in Transylvania, and which solidified many of the vague vampire legends. You will encounter Dracula often in the pages that follow, because his sinister presence has haunted the movies from its earliest times until today.

A different monster who is as ancient as the vampire is the werewolf—the man who is transformed into a wolf when the moon is full. Like the vampire, the werewolf is a creature of the night; when dawn comes, the wolf returns to its human form. The legend of man-turned-wolf was known to the ancient Romans, so it is at least two thousand years old. The same theme is found in African folk tales, and among several tribes of American Indians. Again like the vampire, the werewolf seems to have found his modern home in southeastern Europe; one reason for this is the fact that wolves were common in this region until fairly recent times.

The werewolf legend—and most common beliefs—are unkind to the wolf. While the great majority of people picture a wolf as a wicked beast who kills anything at all, for pleasure more than for food, the real-life wolf has been found to be a self-respecting citizen of the wild who looks after his family, slays only when he and his cubs must eat, and almost never attacks humans. Since this true picture is too tame, the werewolf legend pictures a wolf as a maddened, ravening beast that shows no mercy to anyone and who delights in human blood.

The werewolf of the movies comes into existence when an innocent bystander is bitten by another werewolf. From then on, the man-wolf undergoes a set of unusual changes. The index fingers of his hands become extraordinarily long. The palms of the hands become unusually hairy and begin to itch endlessly. A distinctive five-pointed symbol called a pentagram appears on the werewolf's body, and cannot be removed. But the most remarkable changes of all occur when the moon is full. (Some versions of the legend say the werewolf's fate is also connected with the flowering of the wolfsbane, a plant which blooms under the autumn moon.)

Says the legend: When the moon is full and the wolfs-bane blooms, the man turns into a wolf. His great strength enables him to prowl at large even though efforts have been made to keep him behind locked doors and barred windows. His search is for human victims, and he kills anyone who crosses his path. When daytime returns, the werewolf resumes his human form, with little or no memory of the night's wicked deeds. The man-wolf retains his human form until the next full moon, when he prowls again.

The legend describes only one sure way to kill a werewolf—with a hit by a silver bullet. An ordinary bullet is said to do no harm even if it goes through the werewolf's heart, but the slightest touch of the silver bullet means death. If the bullet strikes when the moon is full, the werewolf will return to its human form as it dies.

Many legends make the werewolf more a figure of

pity than of hatred. The man-wolf cannot help what he does when the moon turns full. And so the silver bullet often is welcome, because the werewolf is horrified at the cruel deeds he commits when in animal form, yet can do nothing to stop himself. Still, the werewolf's gruesome deeds make him a beast to be hunted down and destroyed relentlessly.

There is no work of fiction about werewolves to compare with Bram Stoker's novel about vampirism. Nevertheless, the werewolf began to show up in movies at about the same time as the vampire did, in the early days of silent films, and the subject has remained almost as popular since then. Special effects men and make-up experts take special delights in managing the transformation from man to wolf and back again in the scariest way possible. There are enough variations on the vampire theme—as you will see—to keep the subject going on the screen for years to come.

In addition to these creatures of legend, there is another folk-tale figure of horror who keeps turning up in the movies: the zombie, or walking dead, who was born in the tales told by Africans who were brought to the Caribbean islands to toil as slaves.

The legends describe the zombie as a dead man brought back to life—but life of a particularly unpleasant and frightening kind. The zombie is tireless, working endlessly without food or sleep. He cannot be hurt by any weapon, and he cannot feel pain; when hit by a bullet, the zombie simply does not pay attention. He obeys his master's command without question, and the only way to destroy the zombie is by total elimination. Until that day, he is the total slave of his master—usually a wizard who has created the zombie by a form of black magic or voodoo.

It is easy to see how this legend originated. Working conditions for black slaves often were so terrible that many did come close to being the blindly obedient, endlessly working creatures that a zombie is supposed to be. A dash of superstition helped keep the legend alive even after the end of slavery.

The zombie theme has not been as popular in the movies as the legend of the vampire or the werewolf, perhaps because it is more difficult to make a zombie look terrifying. A vampire can be outfitted with a full set of fangs and a werewolf can be as hairy and toothy as anyone wants, but a zombie usually is just a man with a blank expression. In addition, the zombie is a creature who works hard all day and all night, while werewolves and vampires spend their time not at work but at play— if you care to call stalking human prey a form of play. Children who work in school all day and adults who work in businesses all day would rather watch a vampire at play than a zombie at work; at least, that is what the box office results seem to say. And so zombie movies have not been too successful.

You might think that all these superstitious legends would become more infrequent in modern times, when the rise of science should have put an end to all unscientific tales of monsters. After all, scientists are supposed to be very logical and unsuperstitious, and monsters thrive on fear and lack of logic. But it didn't work that way. Instead, the beginnings of modern science added another kind of villain to the roster of monsters—the mad scientist.

To many people, the power wielded by the scientist is as fearful and mysterious as the supernatural powers described in ancient legends. Almost every day, we read about scientists who accomplish what seems like impossible feats—splitting the atom or building a spacecraft to the moon, for instance. Unless you understand the knowledge that is the source of scientific achievements, it is easy to be frightened by this kind of power.

So while he appears to be a completely new kind of villain, the mad scientist actually is nothing but a modern version of the old-fashioned magician, like King Arthur's Merlin. These magicians, with their mumbo-jumbo, claimed to command vast powers that an ordinary man could hardly begin to understand. The ordinary man shrank back in fear, terrified that these magical powers might be turned against him.

The mad scientist is the same kind of frightening figure. In a way, he is as much a legend as the zombie or vampire. The mad scientist is always pictured as a genius who can accomplish unbelievable things (for example, creating a living man from left-over parts of corpses, or transforming beasts into humans). Sometimes, the mad scientist is a good-hearted creature who does his mysterious experiments to advance human knowledge or to help mankind. Sometimes he is pure evil, creating monsters for revenge, for profit, or out of pure hatred and spite. But one thing you can be sure of when you watch a mad scientist movie: no matter what his motives are, the mad scientist will come to no good. Almost always, he will be destroyed by what he creates.

A few years ago, most scientists would have laughed at that picture. They would have described it as a basic misunderstanding of what scientists do. They would say that scientists are people just like any other, trying to do a good job and not hurt anyone, even though the results of their work sometimes may be misused.

But these days, the old-time image of the mad scientist sometimes seems prophetic. Alarm about the ecological damage man is doing to his world through science and technology has made many people say that scientists must not ignore the effects of their discoveries, but must try to control those effects. Hydrogen bombs and missiles that can destroy whole cities seem like the work of mad scientists. Perhaps, in an odd way, the "mad scientist movies" were trying to tell us something we did not realize: that pure science can, indeed, lead to impure and harmful results.

The most famous mad scientist of all was created long before the movies existed. He was the central figure in a novel written by a young British woman who was married to Percy Bysshe Shelley, one of the greatest poets of all time. More than 150 years ago, when she was just twenty-one years old, Mrs. Mary Wollstonecraft Shelley caused a sensation by writing a novel titled, *Frankenstein, or the Modern Prometheus.*

Prometheus was the legendary Greek figure who stole fire from the gods for mankind and died because of his theft. Mary Shelley, looking at the growing power of science with a poet's eye, conjured up a scientist with an equally daring goal: Dr. Victor Frankenstein, the German nobleman who was determined to create a perfect being by taking parts of human bodies, putting them together, and then bringing a new being into existence.

Frankenstein's dream, and its nightmarish results—the creature was a destructive monster, not a perfect being by any means—caught the imagination of readers at once. Almost every mad scientist since then has resembled Frankenstein. The movies have returned to the theme of Frankenstein and his monster again and again. Usually, Frankenstein movies follow the plot used by Mary Shelley: the man-made monster that proves to be inhuman and vicious, who is destructive and miserable, and who eventually destroys his creator and sometimes himself.

In the 1920s, a different science, archaeology, created a new kind of movie monster: the mummy. It all began in 1922, when a team of archaeologists led by Howard Carter discovered, in the Valley of the Kings, near Luxor, the hidden tomb of King Tutankhamen. Many other tombs of ancient Egyptian rulers were known, but this one was unusual. Somehow, Tutankhamen's tomb had escaped the ravages of tomb robbers, who had stripped every other tomb of all their treasures. Tutankhamen's tomb had such beautiful and valuable objects that the discovery sent a thrill through the whole world. Here was the mummy of a man who had lived nearly three thousand years ago, surrounded by gold, ivory, and beautiful works of art.

This thrill of discovery was followed by a thrill of terror. Somehow, the idea got around that there was a "Curse of King Tut" that would strike down all the people who had invaded the royal tomb. This belief was pure superstition, of course, but the idea of a curse was so exciting that many people half-believed it. In the years that followed, many of the men who had opened the tomb did die. All of them died of natural causes, and most of them were old men. However, those people who wanted to believe in the "curse" accepted no other explanation for the deaths. And, of course, the idea of the mummy's curse was too good for the movies to pass up. Like the mad scientist, the mummy who comes back to life has become a popular figure in monster movies.

Several outstanding films have been made using the mummy theme, and the mystery involved in opening an ancient tomb still provides an excellent framework for horror films.

Finally, there are the animal monsters that can exist only in the movies—the giant beasts of every description that stalk, stomp, slither, and swim across the movie screen. These are the creations of the special effects men, who keep adding to a bag of tricks that have accumulated over several decades of screen trickery. A good special effects man can make you see a dinosaur as big as a mountain or a gorilla as big as a house. He can make an elephant appear to fly through the air, or turn an ordinary ant into a terrifying attacker. It's all done with models, double exposures (shooting two scenes on the same piece of film, so both scenes seem to be happening at once), special sets and many more tricks like these.

In the worst of these films, the monster is obviously just a man dressed up in a funny suit, or an unrealistic model that is maneuvered in front of phony scenery. But the best of these monster movies can bring back extinct dinosaurs with a realism that makes the viewer gasp, or make an impossible beast into a real terror that destroys a city you can recognize.

In recent years, the theme of the giant animal monster has started to merge with the mad scientist theme. Once upon a time, filmmakers had no explanation for the sudden appearance of a giant monster. Now the monsters can be blamed on a scientific experiment that has gone wrong or on a nuclear explosion. But, on the other hand, scientists usually are the heroes of these movies. They always step in at the last moment with a new machine that conquers the monster after everything else has failed.

One of the charms of this kind of monster movie is that you know what you are watching could never really happen. A gorilla as big as King Kong could not exist in real life. Because its bones would not be strong enough to support it, a giant ape would literally collapse of its own weight. So would a giant animal of any other kind, or a giant insect.

Dinosaurs are impossible for a different reason. While the giant dinosaurs you see on the screen actually did exist at one time, no man ever met a real dinosaur. The dinosaurs became extinct more than a hundred million years ago, long before man made his appearance on this planet; modern man did not appear until about one million years ago. So all the movies that show cave men wrapped in skins fighting with dinosaurs are showing you something that never really happened; cave men had to fight saber-toothed cats and woolly mammoths, but never dinosaurs. As for the rest of the sea serpents, octopi, dragons, and assorted other monsters who devastate mankind in horror movies, some of them theoretically could exist, but none of them have actually been found in real life. They owe their movie existence to the wizardry of special effects men who manage somehow to make doll-sized figures tower over actors—on film only.

And that should be a lesson to you, the moviegoer, to pay more attention to the people you don't see on the screen. Most people notice only the actors in movies. You can avoid bad movies and select good ones better if you learn the names of all the other people involved in the making of a monster film.

For example, take the make-up men—the equivalent of special effects men for human actors. Boris Karloff became famous as Frankenstein's monster partly because of his acting ability and partly because of his appearance, which was delightfully terrifying. Credit Jack Pierce, the make-up man who worked for hours every day to give Karloff a strange new face. Pierce did the same masterful job of make-up in a number of other horror movies.

Don't forget the writer of the movie, either. Actors don't make up the words they speak on the screen. A writer has to create those lines, and a convincing plot as well. Writers customarily get very little attention from movie fans, and their names are generally unknown to all but a handful of film experts. Nevertheless, you cannot make a good movie without a good writer.

But the person who should get most of the credit for a good movie is the director. You certainly have heard of Boris Karloff, but just as certainly, the name of James Whale means little to you. Yet it was James Whale who directed *Frankenstein,* the movie that made Karloff famous, as well as the equally terrifying sequel, *The Bride of Frankenstein,* and a number of other excellent horror movies. The same story could be told of *Dracula,* which rocketed actor Bela Lugosi to world-wide fame. That film was directed by Tod Browning, who has a number of great horror movies to his credit, and who has a dedicated following of moviegoers.

What does a director do that makes him so important? He puts all the parts of a movie together into a finished product. Good writing, good special effects, good acting, all still need one more ingredient. The director supplies that ingredient by giving the movie guidance, direction, and pace. He tells the actors how specific scenes should be handled and arranges for the atmosphere of the movie to be just right. In a horror film, that means arranging for the strange shadows, the creaking doors, the artful footsteps in the night, to happen just at the right moments in the film. The director must also insure that each individual scene makes its own point without overdoing it; after all, there is a narrow line between something that is frightening and something that is just laughable. The director keeps the film moving, so that something always grips the viewer's attention. And the director builds the movie to the properly terrifying climax that sends you jumping out of your seat.

No wonder that many moviegoers select their films by the director alone. The number of directors who have made great monster movies is limited, and you should watch for their names. James Whale and Tod Browning have already been mentioned. Even though their films were made thirty years or more ago, they still are regarded as being among the best in the field. Other names of old-time directors to look for include Val Lewton, Fritz Lang, and Curt Siodmak. When you select a more modern film, you should watch for such names as Roger Corman, Terence Fisher, and the great Alfred Hitchcock. This list is far from complete, but it is a starter.

To make the list longer, you might make a point of noting down the name of the director when you see a new movie that you enjoy very much. The next time a movie made by that director comes along, you will be watching for it. In that way, you can build up your own list of favorite directors, and follow their progress. Many movie fans find it fascinating to watch the development of a director from film to film.

But now the lights of the theater are starting to go down, the music is beginning, and the title of the feature is flashing on the screen. Settle back in your seat and prepare to be frightened. The monsters are coming.

The Pioneers

No one knows which was the first horror movie. The early days of the movies, which were also the early days of the twentieth century, were very unorganized. Films were short and simple. At first, moviegoers were excited just to see people and things actually moving on the screen; they did not demand a story until later. But after the initial excitement wore off, they wanted to laugh at comedians, to cry at the plight of pretty girls, and to be frightened by strange creatures and odd happenings. The film producers obliged.

The most famous early filmmaker who specialized in surprising his audiences was Georges Méliès, a Frenchman who started making movies as early as 1896 after a stage career as a magician. At first, Méliès showed only scenes of everyday life. But then he began to discover that tricks could be played with a camera. He made a woman disappear by stopping the camera, having her step off the stage, and starting up the camera again. He created ghostly scenes by using double exposures. He sent men on a trip to the moon by using tiny models. All these tricks are familiar today, but they made Méliès famous in his time. With their supernatural effects, these French films were the beginning of monster movies.

But the place where the horror movie grew to adulthood was Germany. The time was just after the First World War. It really all began with a movie called *The Cabinet of Dr. Caligari,* which was released in 1920. Caligari is still ranked as one of the finest horror movies ever made, although it was filmed more than fifty years ago without sound and with primitive methods. But it still can frighten people. You may never get a chance to see *The Cabinet of Dr. Caligari* outside a movie museum, but all true horror fans should try to see it at least once, to learn how it all began.

Caligari was made immediately after Germany's defeat in World War I. Money was scarce in that conquered country, and the makers of the film used unusual sets that not only provided an eerie effect but also kept costs down: painted backdrops instead of real rooms and outdoor scenery. The backdrops, painted in strangely distorted shapes, added an extra dash of mystery to the plot.

In the movie, an actor named Werner Krauss played the role of Dr. Caligari, an evil hypnotist (on the left in the illustration) who cast his spell over a sleepwalker named Cesare (center), played by Conrad Veidt. Under

1.   *The Cabinet of Dr. Caligari.* Left to right: Werner Krauss, Conrad Veidt, Lil Dagover (DECLA-BIOSCOP, 1920).

Caligari's control, Cesare carries away the beautiful Jane, the heroine, played by Lil Dagover. Enraged townspeople chase Cesare, who is captured and dies. Then, after Cesare's "death," there is a new scene, set in an asylum, which reveals that the whole story actually was just a delusion dreamed by an unbalanced patient.

Despite that closing scene, most viewers were genuinely frightened by *Caligari*. It was like no other movie made up to that time, and it was an instant success when it opened in Berlin. *Caligari* had the same success in other countries, even those where the Germans were still disliked because of World War I. Viewers were impressed by the way that the director, Robert Wiene, made the

unreal seem so real. The strange backdrops and make-up, as well as weird, unexplainable actions, all seemed to make frightening sense—that is, until the lights came on and it was time to return to the real world. In addition to being an excellent movie in its own right, *Caligari* also showed that moviegoers would pay to be frightened. Thus, it opened the way to all the horror movies that followed.

It was just one year after *The Cabinet of Dr. Caligari* was released that the first great movie vampire made his appearance. Once again, German filmmakers were the pioneers. The movie was titled *Nosferatu*. Despite that name, it actually was the first movie version of Bram Stoker's famous vampire novel, *Dracula*. To avoid paying Stoker's heirs any money, the filmmakers changed the name of the film and switched all the scenes from England to Germany. But they did use Stoker's plot with only a few changes.

In *Nosferatu*, the vampire was called Count Orlock, and a frightening creature he was. Orlock was played by an actor with a most appropriate last name: Max Schreck, which means "fright" in German. In fact, the name was so appropriate that it may have been made up to add on extra dash of terror. The make-up man gave Count Orlock staring eyes, clawlike hands and long, pointed teeth that were enough to frighten anyone.

In the film, a young German businessman visits Count Orlock's creepy castle in the Carpathian Mountains and nearly falls victim to the vampire count. With that bit of terror over, Count Orlock packs up his coffins and sets sail to the city of Hamburg. (In the novel, the vampire's

2. *Nosferatu.* Max Schreck (PRANA, 1922).

destination is London.) It is a ghastly ocean voyage on a mysterious ship full of scampering rats, creaking masts, and any other horror you can imagine.

When Orlock reaches Hamburg, a plague breaks out, as a mysterious force brings out an army of rats. But the young man who visited Orlock's castle has escaped back to Hamburg, and he and his young sweetheart realize that the plague was caused by the vampire. At the climax of the movie, the young woman sacrifices herself to kill the vampire, saving the man she loves and the city as well. Her method is simple: knowing that the vampire cannot live in the light of day, the girl uses her charms to prevent Count Orlock from getting back to his coffin before sunrise. As the sun comes up, the vampire is struck by a beam of light and literally shrivels away. As he dies, the castle in the Carpathians also collapses into ruins.

Many fans of horror movies feel that *Nosferatu* does not come up to the level of *Caligari,* mostly because everything is spread a bit thick in *Nosferatu.* In trying to frighten their audiences, the filmmakers always go a little too far, making everything unrealistic. But some of the scenes are excellent. To heighten the feeling of terror, some scenes are shown in negative film—everything that should be black is white, and vice versa. The ghostly ship is also truly chilling. Still, if you see the movie today, you would find much of it laughable or boring. It was not until ten years later, when Bela Lugosi played the role, that *Dracula* really achieved its movie horror potential. Nevertheless, this 1922 film still is a "must" for movie-goers who want to learn all about the art of frightening the audience, if only because it was the first in a long line of vampire epics.

As times grew more difficult in Germany and Hollywood began to flourish, the United States became the film-making center of the world—and that included horror films, of course. One brilliant actor stood out above all others during the era of silent horror films. He was Lon Chaney, whose skill with make-up earned him the name, "The Man of a Thousand Faces."

Chaney had a strange childhood that helped him acquire a taste for the unusual. Both of his parents were deaf mutes, and Chaney had to "talk" to them not with words but with sign language, gestures, and facial expressions. When he grew up and became an actor, Chaney began to specialize in parts that demanded unusual efforts to achieve strange effects. He often suffered to play these grotesque roles. In one film, Chaney played an armless man. He wore a tight strait-jacket that held his arms rigidly against his sides. In other roles, Chaney used similarly extreme devices that made the audience gasp.

In *London After Midnight,* Chaney played a vampire. He achieved his weird appearance by using thin wires which made his eyes bulge, and a set of sharp-pointed teeth which were so painful that he could wear them only for brief periods. In the movie, Chaney played two roles: the vampire who prowled the moors of England, and a Scotland Yard inspector whose appearance was perfectly normal. Viewers who were carried away by the movie's vampire scenes were relieved to learn at the end that those scenes actually were staged by the detective, who was using them to capture a murderer.

In one of his greatest roles, Chaney played *The Phantom of the Opera,* a strange, disfigured musician who lives in the vast, mysterious maze of cellars beneath the Paris Opéra. The Phantom falls in love with a younger singer, and helps to make her a success. But he becomes furious when another singer replaces the girl he loves. The phantom cuts loose the giant chandelier of the opera house, sending it crashing down into the audience. Then he lures the young girl into the cellars, wearing a mask so his face will not frighten her.

But the singer, curious to see the man who has helped her, suddenly tears away the mask—and then recoils in horror. The phantom allows her to return to the surface,

3. *London After Midnight.* The vampire is Lon Chaney
(© 1927 METRO-GOLDWYN-MAYER, INC.).

4. *The Phantom of the Opera.* Lon Chaney (© 1925 UNI-
VERSAL PICTURES AN MCA, INC. COMPANY).

on condition that she tell no one about him. Naturally, she does tell someone—the man she loves. She does not realize that the phantom is listening. The next evening she is carried away by the phantom. But she is saved by a crowd of Parisians who corner and kill him after a chase through the sewers of Paris.

The story is based on a novel by Gaston Leroux, a French writer, and has been remade at least twice, but the Chaney version is still regarded as a masterpiece of terror. Even though the techniques in use then now seem crude and primitive, no one has topped Chaney's ability to make the phantom seem both monstrous and yet somehow human. The viewer fears the phantom and feels sorry for him at the same time. And, of course, Chaney's unforgettable make-up—which also caused him great pain—has never been surpassed.

Lon Chaney was at the peak of his career when the era of sound films arrived. He might have gone on to make many more great movies. But he fell ill and died in 1930, at the age of forty-seven. The movies have not seen his equal to this day.

Three Frightening Men

Do you recognize these two pleasant-looking men? Do you find them frightening? You should, because between them they probably have frightened more people than any other two actors.

The man on the left with the big, quiet smile is named Arisztid Olt. The man on the right with the beaming grin is named William Henry Pratt. You don't recognize those names? Then try these: Bela Lugosi and Boris Karloff, the stage names of these two gentlemen.

Even though it has been many years since either Lugosi or Karloff has made a film, their names should be enough to send a chill down the back of monster movie fans. And their movies will show you why—especially if you are

5. A publicity still of Bela Lugosi (left) and Boris Karloff (right).

lucky enough to see one of these classic films all alone, late at night, on television.

Lugosi and Karloff hardly ever appeared in a movie together, but their names naturally go together. Both achieved fame as screen scarers in the same year, 1931, when two of the greatest of all monster films were released: *Frankenstein,* which featured Karloff as a man-made monster, and *Dracula,* which starred Lugosi as the vampire. Those two films opened the modern era of the monster movie.

Both Lugosi and Karloff had been acting on the stage for many years before 1931, but neither achieved true fame until they set out to frighten people. They did so well at it that they set a pattern for all vampires and monsters to follow. Anytime you imitate a vampire, you really are imitating Bela Lugosi, and anytime you picture Frankenstein's monster, you always see Boris Karloff.

In real life, Arisztid Olt and William Henry Pratt were no more frightening than any other two men you might meet on the street. But when they put on their make-up, stepped on the movie set and began to play their roles, they were unlike any other beings you ever hope to meet. They wanted to scare people, and they did an excellent job of it.

In Castle Frankenstein, located in an eerie East European country, Dr. Henry Frankenstein is busily working on his hobby: building a man in his spare time from parts he has assembled himself. With the help of his twisted little assistant, Hugo, Dr. Frankenstein has put together enough parts to form a man, who he hopes will be a scientific triumph, a creature perfect in every way. (What Dr. Frankenstein does not know is that Hugo has made a mistake, and has used the brain of an executed murderer.) Now the moment has arrived when Dr. Frankenstein will try to breathe life into his artificial man.

That is the start of one of the greatest horror films, *Frankenstein*. The doctor and Hugo have equipped themselves with a laboratory that was up-to-date by the standards of those times. Now that the creature is assembled, the two mad scientists are about to take the next step. Slowly, the lifeless body is lifted to an opening in the ceiling. A storm is raging, and kites strung with wire are being flown to attract lightning. As bolt after bolt of lightning surges through the body it slowly begins to stir. "He's alive!" Dr. Frankenstein shouts in triumph. "He's alive, I tell you! He's alive."

Alas, the scientist soon finds out that the man he has brought to life is far from perfect. In fact, the creature is just the opposite. It is a monster—Frankenstein's monster.

At this point, we pause to remind you that you should not call the monster Frankenstein; that is the name of the scientist who made the monster. The monster itself does not have a name. Call it anything you like, but not Frankenstein.

Aside from being a monster and a box-office smash, the creature is also a masterpiece of movie make-up. Jack Pierce, king of the make-up men at Universal Pictures, worked for hours every day and applied pounds of make-up to turn the pleasant face of Boris Karloff into the inhuman, scarred visage of the monster. Although monsters have come and gone by the dozens since 1931, no one has surpassed the terror of Jack Pierce's creation. When anyone

6.   *Frankenstein*. Boris Karloff is the monster (© 1931 UNIVERSAL PICTURES AN MCA, INC. COMPANY).

wants to show a monster these days, it is almost automatic to draw the flat-topped, sunken-eyed creature with bulging brows and two bolts sticking out of his neck (that was how electricity flowed into the body).

In the movie, Frankenstein keeps the monster chained. But the creature has enormous strength, and he breaks loose and kills Hugo, who has been tormenting him. Then the monster runs away. He has a few quiet moments at the side of a stream with a young girl who is sailing flowers on the water. But the inhuman being cannot tell the difference between the girl and the flowers; he throws her in the

water and she drowns. Then the monster flees, pursued by a crowd of villagers led by Dr. Frankenstein.

The two—the monster and its creator—finally meet on a mountaintop. After a struggle, the monster overpowers the scientist and carries him to a windmill. There they are cornered by the villagers, who set the building afire. As the flames mount, Frankenstein and the monster begin to fight. The monster throws Dr. Frankenstein from a window, breaking his arm. But a crueler fate is in store for the creature. As the villagers watch in grim satisfaction, fire consumes the windmill, and the monster as well. The nightmare started by Dr. Frankenstein's strange experiments is over.

The combination of James Whale's direction, Jack Pierce's make-up, and Boris Karloff's acting made *Frankenstein* a movie that still can frighten viewers after all these years. The film's makers and cast realized what Lon Chaney knew: to be truly effective, a screen monster must be sympathetic as well as scary. At one and the same time, Karloff managed to show the monster's weirdness and its humanity. Even though you are afraid of this clumsy, powerful creature whose strength is fantastic, you still can feel some sympathy when it tries to be a real human being. The film brought to the screen the same gripping characteristics that made Mary Wollstonecraft Shelley's novel of the same name such a success.

Frankenstein was so successful that Universal Pictures came back with a sequel just four years later. Using the same director (James Whale), the same actor as Dr. Frankenstein (Colin Clive), and the same leading man (or monster, Boris Karloff), *The Bride of Frankenstein* added a new ingredient—a female monster, acted by Elsa Lanchester. To everyone's surprise, *The Bride of Frankenstein* was an exception to the rule which says that sequels are never as good as the movies they follow; many critics believe that *Bride* is even scarier than the original *Frankenstein*.

To make the movie, the director and script writer had one big problem to solve: bringing the monster back to life. (Remember, *Frankenstein* ended with the creature dying in the blazing windmill.) Their explanation: the fire had not killed the monster at all. Instead, he had escaped by falling into a water-filled basement. The movie opens as the fire burns itself out, watched by one old couple who remained when the mob left. To their horror, the monster slowly emerges from the charred ruins. Both fall victim to the creature, which then wanders off. A woman's scream at his appearance attracts hunters, and the monster is captured by villagers after a chase. He is tied up, brought back to town, and chained in a dungeon. But (of course) chains cannot hold the monster. In a moment, he snaps them in two and flees once again.

Then comes the only happy time in the monster's existence. He comes to the isolated hut of a blind fiddler. Unable to see the horrible face of his guest, the fiddler takes him in and treats him kindly, even teaching the monster to speak a few words and occasionally playing the violin for the guest's amusement. But this does not last. A visitor sees the monster, a fight begins, and the creature must run for safety again. .

This time the monster has a more sinister encounter. In a cemetery he meets Dr. Praetorius, who is Dr. Frankenstein's teacher of old and who wants to carry on his student's evil experiments. Praetorius brings the monster to Castle Frankenstein. Even though Dr. Frankenstein wants to stop the experiments, Praetorius threatens him until Frankenstein agrees to work toward a new goal: creating a bride for the monster. Together, the two scientists begin to assemble a woman.

Then the remarkable climax. As sparks shoot through the laboratory, the female figure slowly rises. She is a grisly sight, with a dead-white face, staring eyes and a streak of lightning-like white hair. The monster is enthralled by her, but she does not return his admiration; in fact, he re-

volts her. For a few minutes, the monster tries to win his bride in what must certainly be the strangest courtship of all times. But soon he realizes it is hopeless. Now the monster has no hope and no reason to exist. Warning Dr. Frankenstein to leave with his (Frankenstein's) wife, the monster traps Praetorius and the female creature and pulls the lever that blows up the laboratory. As the Frankensteins flee to safety, they look back to see the castle blow sky-high.

The same combination of excellent make-up, acting, and direction make *Bride* as successful as *Frankenstein*. The movie somehow manages to make the eerie love-hate story of the two creatures realistic, when it might have been just laughable. As the title role, Elsa Lanchester is both human and monstrous. As the monster, Karloff actually makes you understand how this strange creature could yearn for a companion. With a minimum of creaking doors, echoing footsteps and other such tricks, the movie still is gripping. Despite its strange plot and cast of characters, *The Bride of Frankenstein* makes you believe (almost) that it might really have happened. And that is the secret of a good horror movie.

Unfortunately, success made the movie's producers go back to the same theme again, and again and again. Because fans wanted to see more monster movies, the monster had to keep coming back to life. But its later appearances were much less believable than the first two, which are considered the best of the lot. "They don't make them that way any more" is a frequent comment of monster movie fans. They are referring more to the old-style plots and acting than to the frightening face of the monster. Anyone can create a horrible being by a heavy application

7.   *The Bride of Frankenstein.* Left to right: Colin Clive, Elsa Lanchester, Boris Karloff, Ernest Thesiger (© 1935 UNIVERSAL PICTURES AN MCA, INC. COMPANY).

of make-up. But it takes more than that to make a good monster movie. *Frankenstein* and *Bride* had that extra dash of horror.

Even though most movie fans will always remember him best as Frankenstein's monster, Boris Karloff acted in a number of other good films during a long and distinguished career. He played a wide variety of roles, enough to prove that he was a good actor even when playing an ordinary man, not a monster. But Karloff's ability to frighten people insured that he would continue to play starring roles in horror movies.

One of his best was made in 1932, between the production of the two Frankenstein movies. It was *The Mummy,* in which Karloff played a peculiar Egyptian archaeologist with two strange interests: he wanted to prevent the opening of the tomb of an ancient Egyptian princess named Ankana, and he kept stalking a beautiful British girl who was visiting in Cairo.

Gradually, the audience learns the archaeologist's weird secret: he actually is an ancient Egyptian who had been in love with the princess Ankana thousands of years earlier. When the princess died, he tried to bring her back to life by using a forbidden ritual. But he was discovered and was mummified alive and thrown into the tomb, with none of the sacred Egyptian rites that would send his soul to rest in the hereafter. So the commoner has lived on through the centuries, never able to rest. Now he wants to prevent modern men from opening and desecrating Ankana's tomb. He is also drawn to the British girl because of her remarkable resemblance to the princess Ankana.

8. *The Mummy*. Boris Karloff is in the case (ⓒ 1932 UNIVERSAL PICTURES AN MCA, INC. COMPANY).

Eventually, the tomb is opened, and the princess's mummy is brought to a museum. The archaeologist is discovered as he kneels beside Ankana's mummy one night, once more attempting to bring her back to life as he had tried in ancient Egypt. Again, the attempt is unsuccessful. Eventually, the archaeologist dies by fire, and the centuries-old curse is ended.

The Mummy had a plot that easily could have been

laughable. But Karloff and director Karl Freund made it believable and spine-tingling. Karloff's burning eyes and ramrod-straight demeanor gave the ancient Egyptian an impressive dignity, and lent realism to the love that had lasted through centuries. *The Mummy* may not achieve the heights of the Frankenstein movies, but Karloff fans will find it well worth seeing.

The same Karloff charm—if that is the right word for the ability to make fright both realistic and enjoyable— shows up under different coats of make-up and through a variety of plots. Among other roles, Karloff donned Oriental make-up to play the sinister Chinese villain in *The Mask of Fu Manchu*. People go to see this movie more as a museum piece than as a real horror movie these days. Fu Manchu was out to conquer the world, and he had all sorts of slaves and machines to help him (kind of a James Bond in reverse). Somehow, he never made it because the hero was always smart or lucky. The movie is fun if you do not take it too seriously.

You might also catch Boris Karloff as *The Man They Could Not Hang* (a scientist who comes back to life to avenge himself on those who condemned him to death), *Die, Monster, Die,* and *The Man With Nine Lives,* among other films. While none of these movies is particularly earthshaking, Karloff always gave a creditable, honest performance. He gave a good many enjoyable chills to a lot of people and could always be counted on to give the best performance possible. As man or as monster, Boris Karloff was an excellent professional.

It is late at night at Castle Dracula, deep in the heart

of Transylvania. Jonathan Harker, a young Englishman, has just arrived at the castle to discuss business with its owner. Already, Harker is feeling uneasy. For one thing, the stagecoach driver who dropped him off at the crossroads drove off as quickly as he could, without a word. Then the carriage that took Harker from the crossroads to the castle had a strange driver indeed—a man who disappeared when the carriage stopped, leaving only a bat to flap off into the night. The castle itself is not a place to make anyone feel cheerful. It is dark and empty, almost in ruins, choked with cobwebs. As Harker looks around him uncomfortably, he hears footsteps on the staircase, and sees a tall figure gliding slowly down the stone steps. As the figure nears the bottom, slashing at the cobwebs that bar its path, it stops. A distinguished-looking man in impeccable evening clothes turns his hypnotic eyes on Harker and speaks: "I am—Dracula."

That is the opening scene of *Dracula,* one of the most famous monster movies ever made. The figure coming down the stairs is Bela Lugosi, playing the vampire Count Dracula, and those three words he spoke were enough to open an era in screen horror.

Lugosi was made for the part of Dracula. He already had acted the part on the stage in the play that had been a London and New York hit. His unforgettable accent, his stiff, elegant appearance and his stern, intent face are unforgettable. No screen vampire has come close to equaling the impact made by Lugosi.

Unfortunately, the movie itself could have been better. The opening sequences, which ended with Harker becoming Dracula's victim, were the best in the film. When Count Dracula comes to London, the film tends to be

9. *Dracula*. Helen Chandler (left) and Bela Lugosi (right)
(© 1931 UNIVERSAL PICTURES AN MCA, INC. COMPANY).

rather talky and slow-moving. The viewer can work up
some chills as Dracula stalks his victims (usually beautiful
young women, who somehow almost always are asleep in
white nightgowns), but more imaginative direction could
have scared people a lot more.

But no one doubts that without Lugosi, the film would
have been a lot worse. Above all, he seemed to be a vampire who truly lived for his work, going after fresh blood

and lovely young throats with a zeal and spirit that were impressive. The moviegoer never has the same sympathy for Dracula that he occasionally does for Frankenstein's monster, but Bela Lugosi's vampire wins a respect that the monster could never earn. The monster is terrible when he is aroused. But you would much rather meet him in a dark alley than the merciless (and always thirsty) Count Dracula.

Despite his murderous habits, Lugosi had attractions for women fans. In the years of his successful frights, he got hundreds of fan letters a week. Most of the mail came from women, who were intrigued by a man who could be both horrifying and charming at the same time.

Like Karloff, Lugosi found that a single exposure of the monster he had created was not enough. In 1935, Lugosi was back in a movie called *The Mark of the Vampire,* which gave him more fresh throats to attack. Unhappily, this was one of those sequels which does not come up to the original. Other Dracula movies followed, and the vampire remains a screen standard. But many fans believe the high (or low) spot was hit with the very first picture, and with the first ten hair-raising minutes of that picture.

Even more than Boris Karloff, Bela Lugosi is identified with one role, the vampire in *Dracula*. One reason is that Lugosi never quite achieved the success that Karloff did after playing that role. After his triumph as Count Dracula, Lugosi made a number of horror movies, but his career was something of a disappointment. The movies generally were not too good; most of them relied more on heavy make-up and crude effects to make the monsters look

frightening than on realistic plots and believable characters. Still, there were good moments for those who followed Lugosi through the years.

One excellent, scary movie in which Bela Lugosi played
a relatively minor role was *Island of Lost Souls,* which
was based on a novel written by H. G. Wells. In the movie,
a young American (played by actor Richard Arlen) finds
himself stranded on a small, out-of-the way island which
is ruled by a mysterious Dr. Moreau, a juicy part played
to the hilt by the noted actor Charles Laughton. Strange
screams and grunts are heard echoing through the night,
and the odd-looking servants shrink from any mention of
the sinister "house of pain" operated by Dr. Moreau.

As time passes, the American begins to learn the eerie
truth. Dr. Moreau is a mad scientist who was forced
to leave his native country because of public horror about
his evil experiments, in which he tried to cross animals and
humans. Now he is carrying on those experiments again,
with frightening success. The servants in the house are
products of those experiments. So is the beautiful but
strange young woman who finds the young American at-
tractive. Near the house is a more sinister group of Dr.
Moreau's creations: a group of half men, half beasts who
are kept under control by a hairy leader—Bela Lugosi,
cleverly made up.

The film's best moments include those in which Lugosi
leads the pack of man-beasts in a recitation pronounced
by Dr. Moreau to keep them in order: "What is the law?"
"Not to spill blood, that is the law." "Are we not men?"
The answers, given in peculiar grunts, are truly chilling.
(In the illustration, the whip-wielding Dr. Moreau is
holding off a group of man-beasts led by Lugosi, the creature in the middle.)

Eventually, Dr. Moreau meets poetic justice. His creatures, enraged by his treatment, revolt and carry him off to the house of pain. The young American, escaping in a boat, hears the screams of the Island of Lost Souls echoing in his ears, but never looks back.

Less successful than *Island of Lost Souls* was *The Ape Man,* made in 1943, in which Lugosi played a mad scientist who was transformed into a not-very-convincing hybrid between man and beast. Most critics prefer to remember Lugosi in his role as Dracula, and in other horror movies, such as those in which he and Karloff starred: *The Black Cat,* a tale of two competing villains; *The Raven,* in which Lugosi played a mad surgeon and Karloff his assistant; and *Dracula's Daughter,* which was not bad for a sequel. Despite the low spots in his career, Lugosi had enough high spots to be remembered for a long time to come.

In 1941, a new screen monster man joined Karloff and Lugosi. He was a second-generation merchant of fright: Lon Chaney, Jr., son of the famed "Man of a Thousand Faces." Christened Creighton Chaney, the son changed his name to Lon when he became an actor. For years, he had little success, getting only minor roles in Hollywood. His first fame came when he gave a memorable performance as the physically powerful but mentally dull Lennie in the movie *Of Mice and Men* in 1939. Two years later he was given the leading role in *The Wolf Man,* which was released just as the United States entered World War II.

The Wolf Man started Chaney on a new career in horror. Once again, make-up man Jack Pierce claimed part

10. *The Island of Lost Souls*. Bela Lugosi (middle, left), Charles Laughton (right) (© 1933 PARAMOUNT PICTURES).

of the credit for the yak-hair outfit that turned man into a hairy, toothy beast that no one would want to meet in a full moon.

Chaney's role in the movie was that of Lawrence Talbot, a college student and son of a wealthy landowner who has just returned home from school. Strolling through the woods near his father's Balkan estate one night, Talbot sees a young girl being attacked by a werewolf. When he goes to the girl's aid, Talbot is bitten by the werewolf— and so he becomes a werewolf himself. (The werewolf who bites Talbot, incidentally, is played by Bela Lugosi.)

Talbot commits several murders in his wolf form during the full moon. Finally, an old gypsy woman tells him the truth he has begun to suspect. The gypsy shows Talbot the dread five-pointed marking, the pentagram, on his body, and tells him that only a silver bullet, or another silver object, can kill him and thus end his wolfish career of murder.

Revolted by what he has heard, Talbot tries to persuade others to stop him from killing. But no one will listen to him. The end comes when Talbot attacks his own father and is clubbed to death with a silver cane. In a peculiar way, it is a happy ending for the unhappy werewolf.

The Wolf Man rates high on the monster fright scale. Fans appreciate its opening moments, when this macabre poem appears on the screen:

Even a man who is pure in heart
And says his prayers by night,
Can become a wolf when the wolfsbane blooms
And the moon shines bright.

The mist-covered forests of the Balkans, the impressive transformation of man into wolf, the good acting by the rest of the cast helped make *The Wolf Man* a success— even though many critics believe the movie ranks a shade below *Frankenstein* and *Dracula*.

For Lon Chaney, Jr., *The Wolf Man* was the start of a frightening career. Even though the werewolf was dead, its success at the box office insured that it would be brought back to life again for future frights. And since Chaney could scare people, his monster future was secure.

But in many ways, *The Wolf Man* was something of a high point in Chaney's career. Like Lugosi, he was to play in many monster movies over the years, but many of them were poorly done. The career that had started so promisingly with *Of Mice and Men* tailed off disappointingly. Still, Chaney made enough good movies, and had enough good moments in not-so-good films, to be remembered approvingly by many fright fans.

In 1943, someone at Universal Pictures had a bright idea: if one monster makes a movie scary, two monsters will make it at least twice as terrifying. The result of that thought was a movie called *Frankenstein Meets the Wolf Man,* which brought together Lon Chaney, Jr., as the wolf man, and not Karloff, but Bela Lugosi as Frankenstein's monster. As the illustration shows, Lugosi used the same Jack Pierce make-up as Karloff had used, but with less effective results. Most people who have seen the original *Frankenstein* found Lugosi's monster a weak substitute.

The makers of horror movies were used to reviving monsters who had died for sure in previous films, so the plot

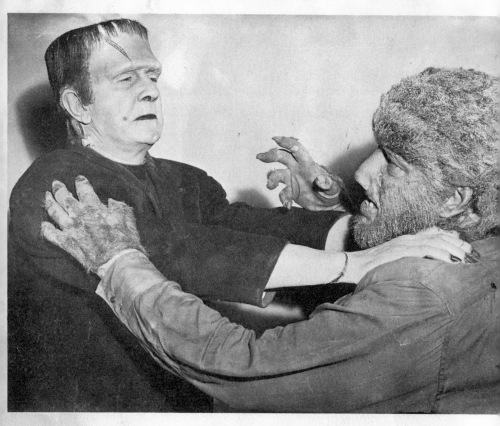

12.   *Frankenstein Meets the Wolf Man.* Bela Lugosi (left), Lon
Chaney, Jr. (right) (© 1943 UNIVERSAL PICTURES AN MCA, INC.
COMPANY).

did not even try to explain how Lawrence Talbot, the
werewolf played by Chaney, had come back to life. The
movie started with Talbot alive again, still a wolf man,
still consulting the same gypsy fortune teller. This time she
tells him that there is only one man who can help him—
Dr. Frankenstein, naturally. Going to Frankenstein's village, Talbot finds that the doctor and his monster have
perished in flames (naturally). What to do now? Before
Talbot can decide, the full moon arrives, and with it his
transformation into a wolf. On one of his nighttime visits,

the wolf man is chased by villagers. He stumbles into the ruins of Frankenstein's laboratory. There he finds the monster, who is frozen solid in a block of ice.

Talbot thaws the ice, but finds that the monster is not much help. Frankenstein's daughter, who is visiting in the village, proves to be of more value. She agrees to send her father's diary to a friend, Dr. Mannering. The hope is that Mannering will learn Frankenstein's secrets, destroy the monster and then help Talbot shake the curse of the werewolf.

Unfortunately, Dr. Mannering picks up Frankenstein's bad habits by reading the diary. He restores the monster to full strength—just during the full moon, of course. That leads to a fight which Universal proclaimed as the "battle of the century": werewolf against monster, going for each other with no holds barred in the mad scientist's laboratory.

The fight ends in a draw. Instead of waiting to see who wins, the villagers blow up a dam, flood the laboratory, and sweep both creatures away to destruction (until the next film, that is). Mannering and Frankenstein's daughter escape to a new future.

The movie has its moments, including a good performance by the beautiful Ilona Massey as Frankenstein's daughter, and effective acting by Patric Knowles as Mannering. Unfortunately, the film started a trend that was to hurt the quality of monster movies in the years that followed.

That trend was multiple monsters. Since the public liked seeing two monsters battle, filmmakers kept adding monsters, until you could see a wolf man and Frankenstein's monster, a vampire and a mummy, or any combination that caught the producer's eye. There is a thin line between being frightening and being funny, and too many of these films crossed that line. No one would ever think of laughing at Lugosi's Dracula or Karloff's monster, but too many of the later "monster rallies" could hardly send a chill down anyone's back. Instead, the moviegoer is more likely to chuckle at the sight of all those monsters. It was a sad way to end an era.

The Big Beasts

In 1929, Merian C. Cooper, a maker of documentary movies, went to Africa to shoot scenes for an adventure film. While he was there, Cooper conceived the idea of a movie whose central figure would be a giant gorilla. He outlined some specific scenes for the film—the gorilla would fight a giant lizard, and then would run wild in a city before his violence was ended. Cooper even invented a name for the gorilla: Kong.

For two years, Cooper did nothing with his idea. But in 1931, when he went to work at RKO Studios, Cooper was able to convince David O. Selznick, who was head of production there, that the gorilla movie would be a success. He even found the man who would insure success:

Willis O'Brien, who already was famous for his special effects that had brought dinosaurs and other outlandish beasts to the screen.

O'Brien had a special technique which he had perfected in a 1925 silent movie, *The Lost World*. He had used small models of dinosaurs with movable joints. By shooting one frame, moving the models slightly, shooting another frame, moving the models again—over and over, with great care —O'Brien got film on which these beasts actually walked, ran and battled to the death. As a test run for the new movie, Cooper and O'Brien made a model of a gorilla and shot a short film using the same technique. It was so impressive that they got the go-ahead for a full-length film.

Making the movie was hard work. The "giant" gorilla, Kong, in most scenes was just a 16-inch-high model that was filmed against special backdrops. The models used in the film were works of craftsmanship, with limbs, eyes and a mouth that moved realistically; for some scenes, detailed models of dinosaurs were used. The technicians would shoot one frame, move the models, then shoot another frame. After ten hours of work, the result was no more than 25 feet of film, enough to fill only 30 seconds on the screen.

For scenes with the human actors, O'Brien used a number of techniques. Sometimes he had the heroine, who was played by actress Fay Wray, held in a giant ape hand that was built to be 8 feet long. Sometimes O'Brien combined live actors with the miniature models by special projection methods. Some of his other methods remain a secret to this day.

King Kong was finally ready for release in 1933. It was an instant smash hit, holding audiences spellbound by the

13.   *King Kong.* (1933 COPYRIGHTED—RKO RADIO PICTURES A
DIVISION OF RKO GENERAL, INC.).

realism of its scene. The plot even worked up some sympathy for the giant gorilla, who was jokingly described as "the tallest, darkest leading man in Hollywood."

By today's standards, the plot of *King Kong* is slow-moving and crude. The film starts as a movie producer, Carl Denham (played by Robert Armstrong), sets off for mysterious Skull Island, off the coast of Africa, to film a mysterious creature which legend says lives there. Once on the island, the producer and his crew fall afoul of the inhabitants. Just as Fay Wray is about to be sacrificed to King Kong, the huge gorilla makes his first, frightening appearance, snatching up the girl and lumbering away.

Then begins one of the most breath-taking sequences in the movie, as Denham and his men chase Kong through a series of unbelievable perils. Kong kills a dinosaur in a fierce battle, he shakes men off a log bridge one by one like ants, and he dangles the hero at the end of a string like a Yo-Yo—always holding onto the beautiful actress, who obviously has captured his gorilla heart.

Finally the producer subdues King Kong with sleeping gas, and brings him back to New York for exhibition. On opening night the flashbulbs of newsmen's cameras enrage Kong. He breaks his chains and is off on another rampage. It is another masterful sequence, showing a giant gorilla on the loose in a great city. Kong tramples walls, destroys an elevated train, and causes panic. Meanwhile, the actress has been taken to a hotel room by the hero. As they give thanks for their safety, the huge, staring face of Kong appears in the window. Sweeping the hero aside, Kong grabs the screaming actress (the director told Fay Wray to scream as long and as loud as she could, and she did just that) and carries her away.

The next morning finds Kong on top of the Empire State Building, which had just been completed as the world's tallest structure. In the film's climax, fighter planes are called in as a last resort. They buzz around the bewildered gorilla like flies, pouring bullets into his body. Kong slumps, puts Fay Wray on a safe ledge, then falls to his death. His epitaph, spoken by Carl Denham to a policeman: "'Twas Beauty killed the beast."

By general agreement, *King Kong* is the best movie of its kind ever made. Even though some of the scenes look odd by today's standards, O'Brien's special effects have never been bettered. But that was not all. Kong was more than just a bundle of tricks. He manages to have a personality. The moviegoer watches as Kong becomes entranced with the beautiful actress, sees the gorilla enraged at his enemies, even sympathizes as the beast is killed. In the excitement of it all, many viewers forget that Kong is not real. Once the action starts, *King Kong* is as exciting today as it was in 1933.

Naturally, the success of *King Kong* at the box office called for a sequel. This time, however, the producers could not bring the monster back to life, King Kong had been killed too effectively for that—a fall off the Empire State Building is too much even for the world's largest gorilla. The next alternative was to invent a son for Kong, and that is exactly what the producers did.

But *Son of Kong,* which was released just a short time after the first hit, did not work out too well financially. One big reason was the great work done by Willis O'Brien in *King Kong.* Even though the special effects in *Son of*

14   King Kong atop the Empire State Building. (1933 COPY-
RIGHTED—RKO RADIO PICTURES A DIVISION OF RKO GENERAL, INC.).

Kong were just as good, they could not possibly top the original. *King Kong* was too fresh in the public's mind for a sequel to succeed.

And Kong's son turned out to be just a pale shadow of his father—a smaller, white gorilla who wanted to play almost as much as he wanted to fight. The plot of the movie followed the original Kong story fairly closely. This time, Carl Denham leaves New York secretly, because he cannot pay for the damage caused by King Kong's rampage. After beating about the Pacific for sometime, Denham hears of Kong's son and finds him. Then follow some of the same kind of scenes that had thrilled audiences in

King Kong. But this time, most audiences just yawned. *Son of Kong* never grew up to be the ape that his daddy was.

Some years later, Willis O'Brien had another try at the same theme, in the 1949 movie, *Mighty Joe Young.* The director of the two Kong movies, Ernest B. Schoedsack, was back to direct the saga of this new giant ape. This time, the gorilla was even smaller (about 10 feet tall) and even tamer than Kong's son. In the movie, Joe Young is the pet of a beautiful girl (played by Terry Moore) who lives in Africa. He is so friendly that a few bananas keep him as a household pet. When an American cowboy visits Africa and falls for the girl, she is persuaded to take Joe Young to the United States for exhibition.

You know what happens. On opening night, Joe Young is quite the opposite of the snarling, hateful King Kong— at first. He appears on stage holding the girl and a piano in the air while she plays the gorilla's favorite song, "Beautiful Dreamer." But once again, the gorilla becomes frightened by the noise and lights, and breaks loose; the scene where a screaming audience fights to get away while Joe Young wrecks a night club and frees the animals in a menagerie, is the best in the movie.

The police hunt the gorilla down fairly easily, and prepare to kill him, even though the girl pleads that he is only misunderstood. To save Joe, the cowboy hires a van and arranges the biggest kidnaping (or apenaping) of all times. As the police close in, Joe Young stops to save some orphans who are trapped in a burning building. This proof of his good nature wins his release, and he goes back to Africa and happiness. It is all rather sticky.

While *King Kong* was a movie that terrified adults, the

15. *Son of Kong.* (1933 COPYRIGHTED—RKO RADIO PICTURES A DIVISION OF RKO GENERAL, INC.).

two sequels are really for the young in heart. Mighty Joe Young has none of the menace of Kong. He is enjoyable, but not unforgettable like Kong, the greatest ape of all.

Over the years, even before King Kong and up to the present day, the gorilla remains one of the most popular movie menaces. Curiously enough, these giant apes are really quite gentle if left alone in their jungle homes; they eat vegetation and not meat, and they will not harm a human unless they are attacked. But their burly build and ferocious looks make them natural movie monsters. Movie-makers of all countries have used fake gorillas of every size and in every imaginable plot.

Of course, the skill with which gorilla movies are made varies quite a lot. Just for fun, there is the gorilla menace in an episode from an old-time serial, *Tim Tyler's Luck*. It is fairly obvious that this gorilla is an actor wearing a monkey suit. The actress who is being "carried away" is also obviously having a hard time looking frightened; it might help if her spotless clothes were mussed or dirtied just a little, or if the scenery did not look so well-bred. Even the gorilla's fur looks a trifle mangy. Still, it is good clean fun for those who fancy runaway gorillas.

At the other extreme is the huge gorilla in a Japanese movie, *King Kong Vs. Godzilla*. The gorilla is frightening, all right—much too frightening, in fact. It is too big and too inhuman to have the same personal impact that the original King Kong did. This film brought King Kong back to life as part of a series of movies whose star was the lizard-like Godzilla, a durable monster who always survived whatever was thrown at him by the army, navy, and

16.   *Tim Tyler's Luck.* (1937).

inventive scientists. Godzilla always amazes the actors in his latest movie when he heaves himself up out of the sea and begins to trample the scenery into smithereens. City after city in Japan is smashed into ruins in these movies, whose special effects are excellent. But the monsters created by the Japanese filmmakers, while technically perfect, often fail to capture anyone's imagination or sympathy. What they do is entirely predictable, from the moment they appear until the last minutes of the picture, when they are beaten off until the next time.

17.   *Rodan.* (TOHO, 1957).

It is interesting to watch Godzilla stamp a city into splinters under his giant feet, or Rodan rise from the waves, and fascinating to watch the latest developments produced by the special effects men. But somehow, it isn't the same as watching King Kong, who had a real personality and could always surprise the viewer.

As the skills of moviemakers have improved, the creation of any monster, no matter what size or description, has become almost routine. At the same time, the plots of monster movies have tended to slip into a rut. Almost any time

18. *It Came from Beneath the Sea.* (COLUMBIA, 1955).

you go to see a monster film these days, you know pretty well what to expect.

In many of the movies, the monster is created as the result of radiation from atomic bombs. This theme is especially common with the Japanese, who must live with the memory of the atomic bombs that were dropped on their country during World War II. Rodan (top), an indescribable sea reptile, is one of these radiation-spawned creatures.

In other cases, the monster is a well-known animal blown up to supernatural size by an unknown cause, as with the American-made octopus in *It Came from Beneath the Sea* of 1955. No matter what, the monster is out to get the human race, either because it has been attacked by people or because it is just plain mean. Buildings are crumpled, people are trampled, and the military is called in to fight the crisis.

Invariably, the armed forces turn the best of their weapons against the monster, but it doesn't do any good. Unlike King Kong, who suffered and died from just a few machine-gun bullets, the new breed of monsters just laughs as bullets, bombs, flames, and any other missile bounces off harmlessly.

That gives the hero his opportunity. Either working alone or with a beautiful girl scientist to help him, the hero comes up with an ingenious scheme that takes advantage of the monster's only weak point. That invention always comes just at the nick of time, as the monster closes in for the kill. The climax of the movie comes as the monster moves in with destruction in his eyes. The streets are full of crowds of people, streaming away to safety, screaming as they go. Women cry, men faint, and the generals throw up their hands. The hero watches tensely, then gives the signal. The secret weapon—whatever it is—is unleashed. For a moment, nothing happens. Then, slowly, the monster stops. Soon, he is retreating. Sometimes the producer even allows the monster to die. But usually, the beast just vanishes into the sea, not to appear again until the next sequel.

In movies featuring dinosaurs (as in *Dinosaurus,* made by Universal in 1960), there are two alternatives: the heroes either go back in time or find an unknown island where time has stood still. The technical excellence of such films often is enough to make you believe that the dinosaurs still survive, as you watch them fight bloodily among themselves while the men cower in fear. Then the dinosaurs turn on the human visitors, who wage amazingly realistic battles against these extinct giants. In the end, the unknown island may be destroyed by volcano or sink into the sea, while the heroes escape at the last moment.

Despite this predictability, monster movies remain favorites of filmgoers. It is fascinating to see the pictures from textbooks come to life through the expert work of filmmakers who can create a dinosaur as realistic as any that ever thrashed across the earth's surface 100 million years ago. At the very least, these movies are good clean fun, and audiences demand an endless supply. And so the monsters keep on coming to your neighborhood theater.

A Miscellany of Monsters

The Wolf Man was the first hit about werewolves, but it was not Hollywood's first try at the subject. In 1935, when movie monsters were riding high with the success of Frankenstein, King Kong, and Dracula, Universal Pictures decided that man-into-beast could also be a box-office attraction. And so was born *The Werewolf of London.* A distinguished stage star, Henry Hull, was selected for the starring role, and once again, Jack Pierce was chosen to create the teeth, hair and pointy ears that would make the werewolf properly frightening to those who had already seen the great monsters of the screen.

The plot of *Werewolf of London* was ingenious. It centered around a little-known legend that linked a cure for a werewolf to a flower. The movie starts as a British botanist by the name of Wilfred Glendon (played by Henry Hull) sets off on a voyage to Tibet in search of the fabled flower, which is named the marifesa. Because the marifesa blooms only by moonlight, Glendon must go out after dark to seek it. During his search, Glendon is attacked by a mysterious creature—a werewolf, in fact— and is bitten. Not knowing that the bite has made him into a werewolf, Glendon returns to London, where he tries to make the marifesa bloom in his laboratory.

Then the full moon arrives. Glendon is transformed into a wolf. He prowls the streets and kills a woman. Realizing what he has done, he becomes horrified. He rents a cheap room in a boarding house and locks himself in. It doesn't work. When the moon is full again, man becomes wolf and kills once more.

Now Glendon is desperate to have the marifesa bloom, so that he can be cured by the blossom. But he knows that someone else wants the rare flower: an Oriental scientist named Yogami, who has visited Glendon to tell him about the marifesa's miraculous power. Yogami wants the flower because he, too, is a werewolf—the very werewolf who bit Glendon in the first place. (Yogami was played by Warner Oland, an actor who achieved fame by playing Charlie Chan, the Chinese detective, in a long series of mediocre mysteries.)

Inevitably the showdown comes. When the marifesa blooms, Yogami steals the blossom. It is the full moon, and Glendon again is transformed into a werewolf. Unable to cure himself because the flower has been stolen, he finds himself with the murderous urge of a movie wolf (quite different from the moderate behavior of a real wolf). To

19.   *The Werewolf of London.* Henry Hull (top) (© 1935 UNIVERSAL PICTURES AN MCA, INC. COMPANY).

his horror, Glendon finds himself attacking his own beautiful young wife. Before he can kill her, Glendon is shot by a silver bullet—a sure way to kill a werewolf. As he dies, the wolf turns into a man again. Glendon has just enough time to gasp a few last words of regret before he dies.

On paper, the plot is convincing enough and critics speak highly of many scenes in *Werewolf of London*— including Glendon's Cockney landlady, whose terror about her mysterious tenant was highly amusing. Despite this praise, the movie was not a success. Henry Hull was not the convincing monster that Lugosi or Karloff was, and that contributed to the film's failure.

Another reason was the success of an entirely different movie, a new version of Robert Louis Stevenson's classic story, *Dr. Jekyll and Mr. Hyde,* which starred Fredric March and had been released only a short time earlier. That film also featured a man who turned into a monster, and it was a smash hit. The feeling in Hollywood was that the public was getting tired of half-men, half-monsters, and wanted to see all-out monsters like Dracula and Kong. It took six more years and much hairier make-up for Lon Chaney, Jr., to turn a werewolf into a box office triumph.

As has already been mentioned, the standard rule in Hollywood is that one good movie deserves another—except that the second movie usually is not as good as the first. That is because a good movie has just the right combination of talent—the right director, the right writer, the right actors. A sequel usually fails to match that perfect combination no matter how hard it tries. You have seen some exceptions to that rule, such as *The Bride of Frankenstein,* but the rule does hold good in most cases.

Son of Dracula, released by Universal in 1943, was one of the exceptions. It starred Lon Chaney, Jr., in the role of Count Alucard (spell it backwards to learn his secret) and actress Louise Allbritton as his lovely vampire assistant. Director Robert Siodmak achieved a good air of terror in the scenes showing Alucard prowling through the foggy streets of London, involved in efforts to bring his lady love under his control. One notable feature of the film was the death outlined for Count Alucard: he returns to his coffin after a busy night on the town, only to find it in flames. When the coffin goes, so does Count Alucard.

Although critics gave *Son of Dracula* good reviews, most of them thought that the original *Dracula* was better. Lugosi obviously was a vampire who loved his work—a Count who can hardly wait to sink his fangs into a juicy neck after a long, hard day in the coffin. Lon Chaney, Jr., on the other hand, was a respectable vampire, but he did not radiate the same gleeful menace as Lugosi. Instead of wanting to attack a throat, it seems to be more a matter with him, or something he does because it is expected of him. Still, *Son of Dracula* has its share of chills for the terror-lover.

A not-so-bad remake, *The Phantom of the Opera,* was done again by Universal Pictures in 1943, eighteen years after the famous silent version starring the elder Lon Chaney. This time, the movie was far from silent—in fact, the critics complained that instead of concentrating on terror, the film spent too much of its time listening to the singing of its two romantic stars, Nelson Eddy and Susanna Foster. The Phantom in this version was played by Claude Rains, who was an excellent actor but who did not have the unequaled mastery of fright that Lon Chaney did. Wisely, Rains did not try to outdo Chaney's make-up. Instead, he wore a mask that hid his face for almost all of the movie.

The plot was pretty much the same, except that Rains played a composer who was scarred by acid and who then descended into the cellars of the Paris Opéra as the Phantom. Even in his bitter self-exile, the Phantom works to make an opera star of his pretty, talented young daughter. There is the same theme of jealousy, the same falling chandelier, and the same thrilling hunt for the Phantom through the cellars of the Opéra.

True to the movie remake tradition, *The Phantom of*

the Opera was filmed once again, this time in England in 1962, with actor Herbert Lom playing the horribly scarred Phantom—this time very visible. Most critics believe the latest version was not the match of the first two. But they are waiting. Now that *Phantom* has been remade twice at intervals of about twenty years, another try might be coming up again. If the same rhythm holds, you can expect the fourth version of *The Phantom of the Opera* to appear on your screen about 1981.

Sometimes film critics would just as soon forget about sequels. But movie horror fans are so enthusiastic about monster movies that many of them will go to see a bad film if a good one is not available. And so the sequels keep coming, often with the same old monsters in slightly different plots. That has one advantage: it gives some variety to the horror movie fan and the television stations that delight in showing old movies.

For example, if mummies are your special kind of monster, you have a wide choice of films, including *The Mummy's Curse, The Mummy's Ghost, The Mummy's Hand,* and *The Mummy's Tomb,* not to mention a new version of *The Mummy,* made in England in 1959. The picture on the next page happens to be from *The Mummy's Curse,* made by Universal in 1944 and starring Lon Chaney, Jr., but it could just as well be from any of the others.

You may remember that in the original *Mummy,* Boris Karloff was the starring monster. The later sequels all have brought out a living (?) mummy, heavily bound up in the familiar bandages and fresh from the tomb. Almost

20. *The Mummy*. Christopher Lee (left), Peter Cushing (right) (HAMMER, 1959).

always, the mummy has come back to life because its tomb has been violated by modern archaeologists who scoff at the thought of a curse. Needless to say, the ones who scoff the most are the first to go, and there is a long round of bandaged hands clutching at throats, creaking coffin lids, dark shadows, and other assorted frights before the hero finds a way to dispose of the mummy. The mummy's fate may seem final, but you know that the mummy will rise again for another try in a new monster movie.

Another trend that bothers many horror movie fans is the tendency to play monsters for laughs. One result of that trend was the film titled *Abbott and Costello Meet Frankenstein,* which threw in the Wolf Man for good measure. This film is the end of a long, long line of movies that started off with true horror and ended up making fun of themselves. It is a movie that children may enjoy, but adults probably will not. Just imagine: the monsters who terrified an entire nation now are reduced to being straight men for two movie comedians!

The film had good actors—Bela Lugosi as the monster, Lon Chaney, Jr., as the Wolf Man. But everyone was more interested in the jokes than in terrifying the audience. As far as horror went, *Abbott and Costello Meet Frankenstein* was the end of the line for these monsters. From then on, monster moviemakers and fright-mongers had to start looking for new ideas.

In the mid-1950s, new actors and directors in the good old monster movie style created a new era of chills in both the United States and England. On this side of the Atlantic, a talented director named Roger Corman began making a series of films based on the horror tales of Edgar Allan Poe. The films included *The Pit and the Pendulum, The Fall of the House of Usher, The Haunted Palace, The Masque of the Red Death* and *The Raven.* Much of the time, the movie plot did not have a lot in common with the original Poe story, but the gloomy atmosphere was the same.

Most of these films starred Vincent Price, who managed to be terrifying even when he gave the impression of not quite taking the whole business too seriously. Corman's direction featured much more gore than the old monster movies did, probably on the theory that much more is needed to shock people today than years ago. Still, Vincent Price always keeps the terror under control, sometimes kidding with the plot a bit but always maintaining at least a hint of horror.

Roger Corman still is active in filmmaking, and is branching out to new subjects. He is one of the fastest workers in the business; one of his movies was made in just three days, an unbelievably short time for these complicated years. Corman had finished a movie a trifle early, and so he whipped up another film that used the same sets and many of the same actors. While the Corman-Price movies are not regarded as hitting the same peaks of fright as the classic monster films of the 1930s, they do keep the old tradition alive and vibrant.

On the British side of the Atlantic, a small company named Hammer Films began turning out new versions of the old movie greats. The first remake was *The Curse of Frankenstein,* released in 1957, which was followed the next year by *The Horror of Dracula,* and on and on to this day.

21.   *The Pit and the Pendulum*. Right: Vincent Price (AMERI-
CAN INTERNATIONAL PICTURES, INC., 1961).

22. *The Curse of Frankenstein*. Christopher Lee (on the table)
is examined by Peter Cushing (HAMMER, 1957).

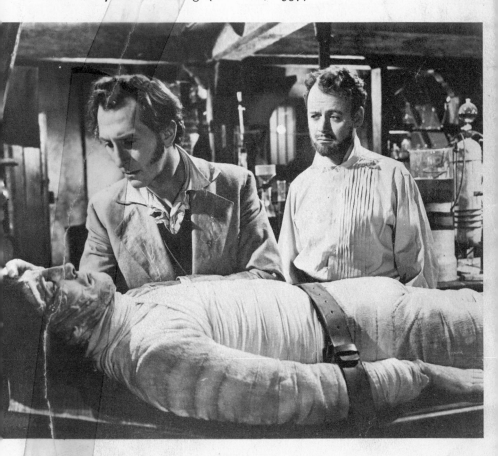

Hammer's favorite director is Terence Fisher, who had two leading actors, Peter Cushing and Christopher Lee; usually, Cushing plays the scientist in these movies, while Lee plays the monster. In the illustration, Cushing, playing Dr. Frankenstein in *The Curse of Frankenstein,* is inspecting the heavily scarred face of his creature, played by Christopher Lee.

Cushing brings a touch of British coolness to his films, always remaining calm even when the worst is happening. Lee suffers from the fact that new make-up has to be created for the old roles (Universal, for instance, has copyrighted the original Frankenstein's monster make-up and protects it fiercely). In *The Curse of Frankenstein,* Lee's gruesome scars and bulging eyeball did not come up to the Karloff monster of old. It was Cushing and Lee again in *The House of Dracula* (with Fisher directing); Lee died a typical vampire's death when he encountered a crucifix and daylight.

The plots of these two films were essentially the same as the earlier *Dracula* and *Frankenstein.* But the new movies are in color, and they give the viewer plenty of blood and other gory details. Gore, and plenty of it, is typical of most Hammer films; the studio piles on as much as it thinks the audience will take. In some cases, Hammer has released different versions of a film for different countries, depending on that nation's taste for gore.

With all the blood, Cushing provides the same stability as does Price. His crisp British sense of authority never wavers. Using Fisher, Cushing, Lee, and other talent it has developed, Hammer is running through the full range of traditional monster themes, from mad scientists to were-

23. *The Curse of Frankenstein.* Christopher Lee (HAMMER, 1957).

24. *Dracula,
Prince of Darkness*.
Christopher Lee
(HAMMER, 1965).

25. *The Curse of the Werewolf.* Yvonne Romain, Oliver Reed (HAMMER, 1961).

wolves. Times may change, but the monsters keep marching on.

American-International Pictures, which released many of the Roger Corman-Vincent Price films, has always had a strong bent for the teen-age market. A young producer by the name of Herman Cohen looked at the combination of millions of teen-age filmgoers, and their taste for monster movies, and came up with a logical product: teenage monster movies. The results of that endeavor include two big box-office hits, *I was a Teen-age Werewolf* and *I Was a Teen-age Frankenstein*. While neither of these films will ever make the horror hall of fame, both of them provided a lot of fun for youthful viewers.

Both films used youth-minded variations on the standard monster movie plots. For example, the teen-age Franken-stein (the monster was the teen-ager, not the doctor) was assembled by a mad scientist from the American branch of the Frankenstein family. This mad scientist used parts of teen-agers only to produce his creature, and the monster had many of the habits of teen-agers, including a keen eye for pretty, young non-monster girls.

The teen-age monster movies proved several points. One is that working conditions have improved greatly in the laboratories of mad scientists. Not only do mad scientists use up-to-date equipment these days, but they also have done away with the cobwebs, bats, and mossy stones that made old-fashioned laboratories unsanitary as well as spooky.

It is also obvious that the monsters of today are much more clean-cut than the old brand. Even though the young werewolf is both long in the tooth and hairy in the best tradition of man-turned-beast, he does look something like a college student who will be back at his books, preparing for the big exam, as soon as the full moon disappears from the night sky.

Basically, these movies played their monsters more for laughs than for chills. But the American-International films did introduce many young moviegoers to the world of monster films. They also served to pave the way for several

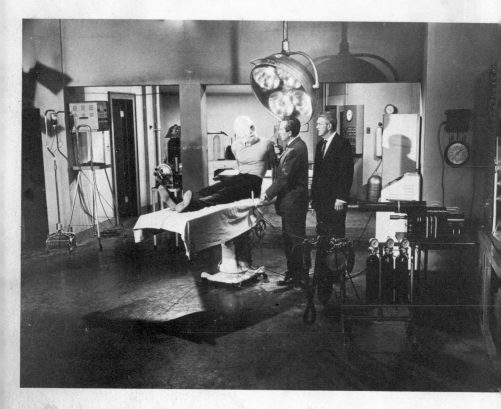

26. *I Was a Teen-age Frankenstein*. Monster: Gary Conway. Scientist: Whit Bissell (AMERICAN INTERNATIONAL PICTURES, INC., 1957).

27. *I Was a Teen-age Werewolf*. Michael Landon (AMERICAN INTERNATIONAL PICTURES, INC., 1957).

television series that have featured monsters. These series still can be seen, in reruns, on many stations.

One series, *The Addams Family,* was based on a weird brood of beings created by a cartoonist, Charles Addams. Another, *The Munsters,* has a father who was the image of Frankenstein's monster, a mother who resembled a vampire, a werewolf son and a grandfather who bore a strong resemblance to Bela Lugosi. The viewer of these two series knows better than to be frightened by these sights; it is all in rather mild fun. Even though Rod Serling has written several series of television shows that set out to terrify the viewing audience at home, television had not had much success with monsters. The exception was a daytime serial, *Dark Shadows,* whose unearthly cast of characters achieved some popularity. But that serial went off the air eventually. The movies still reign supreme in the monster field.

While some filmmakers stick with the old standbys, others are going down new paths of fright. In particular, the age of the atom and of space has given the movies any number of new ways to create blood-curdling monsters. They can come from outer space, from the ocean depths, from the atom's radiation, and from just plain imagination. And they keep coming.

In *The Day of the Triffids,* the villains were vegetable-type creatures who invaded the earth from another planet; the idea of a walking, thinking vegetable is even more frightening than that of an animal monster—usually, vegetables are harder to get rid of than giant animals. A good vegetable monster has seasoned many a modern monster movie.

In *The Creature from the Black Lagoon,* the villain was a kind of super-frog—actually, actor Ricou Browning

28. *The Day of the Triffids.* (ALLIED ARTISTS PRODUCTIONS, INC., 1962).

29.   *The Seventh Voyage of Sinbad.* Kerwin Mathews (COLUMBIA, 1958).

dressed up in an excellently detailed monster suit that might have been just a bit too perfect to frighten actress Julie Adams. Even though the monster is too well groomed for its own good (shouldn't a creature that lives in a black lagoon be dripping with seaweed and barnacles?) is too pretty to look very frightened, *The Creature from the Black Lagoon* was successful enough to spawn a couple of sequels.

Films such as *The Seventh Voyage of Sinbad,* released by Columbia Pictures in 1948, testify that Hollywood's skill with special effects lives on, as you can tell from the realistic duel between a man and a skeleton. The man responsible for the special effects in *Sinbad* is Ray Harryhausen, who is truly carrying on the tradition of Willis O'Brien; Harryhausen was O'Brien's collaborator in making *Mighty Joe Young.* Harryhausen has created equally imaginative special effects for a series of movies including *Jason and the Argonauts* and *The Mysterious Island;* indeed, he also created *The Creature from the Black Lagoon.* Even when the plots of these movies happen to be slightly weak, the special effects are always worth seeing.

And finally, there is the preview of things to come in an Italian movie which was released in the United States under the title of *Planet of the Vampires.* Even when man goes into space in centuries to come, it seems, the monsters of old will be there to frighten him as before—if only in imagination, and even if they are always conquered in the end. Man has come a long way from the dark forests and shadowy caves that were the homes of the first monster stories. But even though we conquer the solar system in ultramodern spacecraft, there still is that deep-down need

30. *Planet of the Vampires.* Barry Sullivan (left) (AMERICAN INTERNATIONAL PICTURES, INC., 1965).

to be deliciously frightened for a few hours, until it is time to come out of the theater into the light of modern day again. Apparently monsters will be with us for some time to come.

Edward Edelson is at present a science editor for the New York *Daily News*. A graduate of New York University, in 1963–64 he was a Sloan-Rockefeller Fellow in the Advanced Science Writing Program at Columbia University. He was formerly a senior staff writer for *Family Health* magazine and prior to that a science editor for the New York *World Telegram* and later for the *World-Journal-Tribune*. Mr. Edelson makes frequent appearances on educational television; for the last several years he has been the science commentator for television coverage of the annual meeting of the American Association for the Advancement of Science. He is the author of *Parent's Guide to Science* and the co-author, with Fred Warshofsky, of *Poisons in the Air*. Mr. Edelson lives in Jamaica, New York, with his wife and three children.

Index

Abbott and Costello Meet Franken-stein, 78
Adams, Julie, 94
Addams, Charles, 90
Addams Family, The (TV series), 90
African folk tales, 8
Allbritton, Louise, 74
American Indians, 8
Animal monster theme, 15–16
Ape Man, The, 47
Arlen, Richard, 46
Armstrong, Robert, 58

Background music, 4–5
Black Cat, The, 47
Black magic, 10
Bride of Frankenstein, The, 17, 36–40, 74
Browning, Ricou, 90–94
Browning, Tod, 17, 18

Cabinet of Dr. Caligari, The, 22–24, 26
Carter, Howard, 14
Chandler, Helen, 44
Chaney, Creighton. *See* Chaney, Lon, Jr.
Chaney, Lon, 26–30, 36, 75
Chaney, Lon, Jr., 47–53, 74–75, 76, 78
Clive, Colin, 36
Coffins, vampire, 6, 7, 8
Cohen, Herman, 86–87

Conway, Gary, 88
Cooper, Merian C., 55–56
Corman, Roger, 18, 78–79, 86
Creature from the Black Lagoon, The, 90
Crucifix, vampire fear of, 7
Curse of Frankenstein, The, 79, 81, 82, 83
"Curse of King Tut" (superstition), 14
Curse of the Werewolf, The, 86
Cushing, Peter, 77, 81, 82

Dagover, Lil, 22, 23
Dark Shadows (TV program), 90
Day of the Triffids, The, 90, 91

Die, Monster, Die, 42
Dinosaur theme, 16, 69
Dinosaurus, 69
Directors, role of, 17–19
Double exposures (two scenes on same film), 15
Dr. Jekyll and Mr. Hyde, 74
Dracula, 8, 17, 24, 26, 33, 42–46, 51, 71, 75, 82
Dracula, Prince of Darkness, 85
Dracula's Daughter, 47
Dragon monster theme, 16

Eddy, Nelson, 75
Egypt (ancient), 6, 14

Fall of the House of Usher, The, 79
Fisher, Terence, 18, 82
Foster, Susanna, 75
Frankenstein, 17, 33–36, 37, 39, 40,
51, 71, 82
*Frankenstein, or the Modern Pro-
metheus* (Shelley), 13
Frankenstein, theme of, 13–14
Frankenstein Meets the Wolf Man,
51–53
Freund, Karl, 42
Full moon, werewolves and, 9

Garlic, 7
German film industry, 22–26
Godzilla monster, 64–67
Gorilla movies, 55–67
Greece (ancient), 6

Harryhausen, Ray, 94
Haunted Palace, The, 79
Hitchcock, Alfred, 18
Holy water, 7
Horror of Dracula, The, 79
Horror tales, primitive times, 1–3, 6
House of Dracula, The, 82
Hull, Henry, 71, 72–73

I Was a Teen-age Frankenstein, 87, 88
I Was a Teen-age Werewolf, 87, 88
Index fingers, werewolf, 9
Island of Lost Souls, 46–47, 48
It Came from Beneath the Sea, 67,
68–69

Jason and the Argonauts, 94

Karloff, Boris, 17, 31–42, 45, 47, 54,
73, 76, 82
King Kong, 55–64
King Kong vs. Godzilla, 64–67
Krauss, Werner, 22

Lanchester, Elsa, 37, 39

Landon, Michael, 88
Lang, Fritz, 18
Laughton, Charles, 46, 48
Lee, Christopher, 77, 81, 82, 83, 85
Leroux, Gaston, 30
Lewton, Val, 18
Lom, Herbert, 76
London After Midnight, 27, 28
Lost World, The, 56
Lugosi, Bela, 17, 26, 31–33, 42–47, 48,
50, 51–53, 54, 73, 78, 90

Mad scientist theme, 11–13, 14
Make-up men, 17
Man They Could Not Hang, The, 42
Man With Nine Lives, The, 42
March, Fredric, 74
Mask of Fu Manchu, The, 42
Mask of the Vampire, The, 45
Masque of the Red Death, The, 79
Massey, Ilona, 53
Mathews, Kerwin, 92
Méliès, Georges, 21–22
Mighty Joe Young, 63–64, 94
Moore, Terry, 63
Mummy, The, 40–42, 76–78
Mummy theme, 14–15
Mummy's Curse, The, 76
Mummy's Ghost, The, 76
Mummy's Hand, The, 76
Mummy's Tomb, The, 76
Munsters, The (TV series), 90
Mysterious Island, The, 94

Nosferatu, 24

O'Brien, Willis, 56, 63, 94
Octopi theme, 16
Of Mice and Men, 47, 51
Oland, Warner, 72
Olt, Arisztid. *See* Lugosi, Bela

Phantom of the Opera, The (1925),
27–30

Phantom of the Opera, The (1943), 75

Phantom of the Opera, The (1962), 75–76

Pierce, Jack, 17, 34, 36, 47–50, 51, 71

Pit and the Pendulum, The, 79, 80

Planet of the Vampires, 94, 95

Poe, Edgar Allan, 79

Pratt, William Henry. *See* Karloff, Boris

Price, Vincent, 79, 80, 86

Prometheus, legend of, 13

Rains, Claude, 75

Raven, The, 47, 79

Reed, Oliver, 86

Romain, Yvonne, 86

Rome (ancient), 8

Schoedsack, Ernest B., 63

Schreck, Max, 24, 25

Sea serpent theme, 16

Selznick, David O., 55

Serling, Rod, 90

Seventh Voyage of Sinbad, The, 92, 94

Shelley, Mary Wollstonecraft, 13, 14, 36

Shelley, Percy Bysshe, 13

Silver bullets, 7, 9

Siodmak, Curt, 18

Siodmak, Robert, 74

Son of Dracula, 74–75

Son of Kong, 59–63

Stevenson, Robert Louis, 74

Stoker, Bram, 8, 10, 24

Sullivan, Barry, 95

Teen-age monster movies, 87–90

Television, 5, 90

Thesiger, Ernest, 39

Tim Tyler's Luck, 64, 65

Transylvania, province of, 6, 8

Tutankhamen, King, 14

Vampire bat, 6–7

Vampire theme, 3, 5–8, 10, 11, 12, 24–26

Veidt, Conrad, 22

Voodoo, 10

Wells, H. G., 46

Werewolf of London, The, 71–73

Werewolf theme, 8–10, 11

Whale, James, 17, 18, 36

Wiene, Robert, 23–24

Wolf Man, The, 47–51, 71

Wolfsbane (plant), 9

World War I, 22

World War II, 68

Wray, Fay, 56, 58, 59

Zombie theme, 10–11, 12